MUSES TO SUSTAIN THE THOUGHTFUL LIFE

Bob Handwerk

Table of Contents

DEDICATION

To my wife Agnes for her support, wisdom, and inspiration.

ACKNOWLEDGMENT

Warm Thanks To

Cliff Carle- my editor; Theresa, my daughter, for her infectious excitement, Burlington Writer's Group, Take Time for Poetry Group, Beloit Men's Tuesday Night Group, Sam Paddock, Curt Lansbery, Jim Templin, my Friends on Facebook

PREFACE

Are you most comfortable in the quiet of the woods, on a beach with the waves gently coming ashore, or relaxing on a park bench in an urban setting? Wherever, whenever, time and space incline you to be thoughtful, you are encouraged to walk hand in hand with these muses and reflect at a pace which enhances the celebration and sustainability of your life.

"Muses to Sustain the Thoughtful Life" is a collection of reflections which has evolved from discussion pieces I prepared for business executives and community leaders who are drawn to exploring philosophical, mind-expanding topics such as cultural mores and religious oriented values. Feedback from blogs over a period of several years leads to multiple requests for the expansion into a format which includes the discussion of how the interrelationship of individual and societies' culture and values are impacted by a diversity of views on nature, family, and religion.

The book's central focus is that of providing the reader with muses designed to assist in a thoughtful self-examination of culture and values, and how these benchmarks determine our life decisions. Scenarios are presented which stimulate individual reflections and calls to action.

In researching this book, I have 2interviewed many successful business leaders who have developed corporate values and manage organizations based on their principles. Additionally, having lived in Europe, the Middle East, and USA, my communications with individuals of various economic and social strata have contributed to a diversity of viewpoints. The opportunity to explore precepts which parallel those of myself as well those which differ, has led me to a broader exploration of global societies' cultures and values. In addition, being exposed to many climactic conditions has been beneficial in learning to recognize and understand some of the subtleties of nature's messages and how they impact life's deliberations and times of celebration.

ABOUT THE AUTHOR

Bob Handwerk is an author, executive coach, and counselor. He has been engaged by leading companies and educational institutions in the United States, Europe and the Middle East. These include: Arabian American Oil Company (Aramco, American Overseas Company, Aramco Services Company), Gilbert/Commonwealth Associates, Deleuw Cather, American School of Warsaw. He currently is president and CEO of the executive consulting firm RLH & ASSOCIATES, LLC.

With expertise in human resource management, he analyzes and writes corporate employee policies, develops management and supervisory training programs, resolves employee –employee conflicts and conducts international wage and salary surveys. He has directed employee selection, policy development, and employee benefit departments. Additionally, he coaches and mentors senior executives staff in such areas as state of the art management techniques, communications skills, and employee selection.

Bob has served on a variety of boards and advisory groups including: Board of

American School of the Hague, Board of Delavan Rotary Club, Executive team of American School of Warsaw, President's Committee for Employment of the Handicapped, and Parish Councils. Notably, he was received an award from the Polish-American Women's Council for promoting Polish -American Relations.

He has written a series of articles for the National Association of Home Builders, has been an editor for Catawba College Alumni Magazine, Sports Center of Catawba newspaper, and various company publications.

Educational degrees are: M. ED from Shippensburg State University and a B.A. from Catawba College. He is also a Certified Professional Counselor.

He is a resident of Delavan, Wisconsin with his wife Agnes.

MEDITATION

I PRAY FOR YOU EVERY DAY

Racks of greeting cards for almost any occasion prominently line the gift shop's entranceway. Clever sketches of flowers, clouds, and dancing angels leap off the card faces. Mundane, simplistic phrases hoping to appeal to the pride we have for our mothers are written in computer generated script. Somehow the cards display an emptiness. The phraseology resounds of automated coldness generated by a software program. Perhaps it is the need to appeal to everyone, everywhere that the uniqueness, feeling quality has been lost? Where are the emotive feelings? The prospective buyer flipping through the cards is lost in a disorganized maze of mindless thoughts.

There is an audience unreached by this commercialization. For many years we've searched for just the right card and the perfect token of our love. Words don't quite capture our thoughts. Now mother is gone. She has been laid to rest and sits at the right hand of our Lord watching over us as she has always done. How do we thank our now deceased mother? How do we recognize her for the life she dedicated to us? The personification of the Virgin Mother is gone forever. Pictures hanging on our office walls last a lifetime. Memories of her voice, the scent of her perfume, the gentle feelings of her touch all remain.

An everlasting tribute is hugging those we love the way our mother embraced us. Even in her final days, each embrace carried the lifelong message of protection, love and commitment. Our mothers watch and pray for us into eternity. A wise mother says, "You are always my child."

Let us pause to hear the heavenly voices of eternal muses as they herald the passage of one generation to the next. These tender sonnets remind us of our mothers praying with us in the nighttime stillness. Each prayer originates from our mother's profound spirituality and beseeches the Creator to keep her children safe and happy.

One of my mother's last words "I pray for you every day" forever hangs in the air. I can see her lying on her death bed reaching out her frail hands to ensure I know how much she has cared. She is omnipotent knowing that by passing along her lifelong prayer that I will accept this lyrical phrase as a necessary guidepost, helping me to ask for divine intervention in being a Christian parent. The phrase "I pray for you every day" surpasses human understanding. A few powerful, beautiful words which mean so very much as they act as a conduit connecting two generations.

Mom, I never told you how wonderful it was to watch you enjoy twenty years of happiness with Bud. He treated you with respect, dignity, and love which you sought in a life partner. You passed these values onto my brother and me. We know that in heaven you pray for us every day. Whenever thrust into difficult, life changing situations, we hear your voice, know your guidance, and pray as you taught us. Therefore we say, "Blessed are thou among women."

GOD TALKS TO US

Worrying can be an all consuming avoidance tactic. This strategy is often an attempt to avoid anticipated, yet not validated potential threats. The dour, pessimistic, drum beating, naysayers are experts at worrying. Hunched shoulders, furrowed brows, shuffling sandals telegraph body language signals that say "I am a committed worrier."

Some see themselves as responsible to carry the weight of the world for everyone, everywhere, all the time. No problem, issue, or threat is too small or immense to be added to their compendium of life's troubles. These human beasts of burden diligently carry their perceived load 24/7. Their psyches are forever fogged with the confused facts of life.

Want to commune with God? This may be as close as it gets. He stands smiling, waiting on the ice for us to come to Him. We hesitantly test the strength of the lake's ice as we approach the area where the ice floes are clashing into each other. Our legs weakening, eyes blurred with tears, we are mesmerized. The transcendence of this moment transforms us into intense, focused listeners. Listening for what? Undefined? Mystical? Unexplainably supernatural, the heavenly fog envelopes us.

We hesitate. Should we consider venturing further onto the ice and into the unknown of nature's living room?

Looking shoreward, we spot a solitary red-winged blackbird tightly clutching the frozen upper limb of a towering, leafless oak. The tree leans forward with its lower branches hovering over the hillside's rocky ledges which surround this ancient lake. Is the bird's presence a happenstance? Out of place on this frigid lake, why is it calling? Suddenly there is a rocket style liftoff. The bird quickly becomes a minute black speck flying at full speed mere meters above the frozen white canvas. This bird, with a lineage spanning generations, delivers a survival message to us of eternal, continuous optimism. We are dependent on those around us for survival.

Loneliness is not an option if we are to share our God-given talents with others. Are we listening? Or do the bird's beckoning sounds fall to the frozen earth unheard? Through the blackbird, nature encourages us to reflect deeper into our inner selves. We are blessed to have this silent time with God when it's just Him, us, and the blackbird in the wooded terrain, which for centuries has adjoined the shores of the lake. A rare opportunity awaits us. Let us follow the bird's example and take a risk by seeking God in places heretofore unknown.

A powerful five letter word hangs suspended in the cold arctic air above the lake. We hear the bird whispering to us as it whizzes overhead. TRUST. The blackbird trusts nature to enable it to survive and procreate. Do we listen to our God even in the most remote, yet beautiful places?

DIRECTION, PURPOSE AND

FAITH

He entered through the restaurant's alleyway door; quietly slide into a darkened corner booth. Alone. His North Face coat strategically hangs on a U-shaped hook to shield him from the view of other patrons. Face down, inches from a plateful of fried Icelandic Cod, the hunched over septuagenarian enjoys the country town's premier Friday night fish fry. Olive tinged skin, scraggly white beard and brooding face combine to say "I am old and feel like a failure, leave me alone." Dressed in a faded, wrinkled, oversized Brooks Brothers shirt with sleeves two inches too long, he emits an aura of someone succumbing to life's tsunami of misfortunes. Incoherent mutterings to himself center around the ever changing weather and decades long deteriorating health. The list includes flat feet, bypass surgeries, failing eyesight, hip replacement. Perhaps the list is much longer.

Meal over, he shuffles from the booth to slowly rise and sit at the far end of the bar. He calls out to the bartender "Miller Lite."

A regular sits down on a neighboring stool and loudly inquires: "What're doin' with yourself, Ned, ,now that you've retired from the mill?"

Nothin', he says, "nothing". " Don't do a damn thing." Questions about the Packers or ice fishing draw grunted responses. Life has evolved into a sad, lonely journey,

Years of inactivity, overeating, carousing, contribute to his appearance of living on the edge near death. Does he spend nights sleeping in the back seat of a rusted out Ford Focus? No one seems to know. Fleshy jaws are swollen red and bowed shoulders communicate the appearance of a thrice beaten boxer. What occurred inside the soul of this once energetic, athletic, successful man?

Nearby, a lively table is occupied by chatty, laughing millennial. Successful entrepreneurs active in their churches and Rotary; they are intent on seeking the next challenge in life. Family and faith are centerpieces of their lives. Each one knows these friends will be by their side when the inevitable storm clouds of life appear. Interestingly, this group holds hands and prays together after the waitress delivers the hearty

17

Midwestern dinners. They are thankful for the food and for each other.

Clustered together at another table, far from the center of the lively repartee, is a quiet, more subdued group. These diners radiate the demeanor and body language of prematurely aging seniors. Conversational topics are negative. Life's failures, problems with the neighborhoods in which they live, and dire predictions about the weather are central themes. Body language is defeatist with heads bobbing in a negative direction during the discussion. Positive vibrations about life's possibilities are absent. As with a movie preview, the precursor of aging appears to be on display. Already these folks are giving up on what has been a lifetime of success, joy, and wholesome family lives.

One wonders which comes first, the physical deterioration of the body or the loss of a zest for experiencing life. What creates the circumstances for some to prematurely cash in their chips and checkout? There is a definable combination of energy, direction and faith which determines life's path. Our deepest inner voice persuasively whispers as we confront life's important junctures. The voice of God is always with us. The rapidly aging man, presently drinking a Miller Lite is a poignant example of living life with a negative focus. This fixation leads to loneliness, grumpiness and a fatalistic attitude towards the future. Many years ago he turned off his internal hearing aid and disregarded God's advice to be thankful for life's blessings. Will he save himself?

In a positive vein, the continuing development of a sense of direction, purpose and faith serve as life's foundation for enriching spiritual regeneration. All of these are priceless. None can be purchased from a local retailer. They are found in our quiet moments of reflection, conversations with God, as well as those times when we share our souls with people we love and trust. The differences between the prematurely aging seniors, the happy clan and the soul who appears completely defeated are clearly observable.

Which do you identify with?

THE THIRD DIMENSION

Nike walking shoes carry the urban trekker through knee-high prairie grass onto the edges of the emerging woodlot. The paranormal combination of hardwoods and evergreens is amazing and confusing. Diamond shaped sun rays randomly dance off the remaining painted leaves on red maple trees. The tree light appears as a psychedelic combination of bright yellow and golden orange. This eerie third dimensional presence focuses on the maple tree even as dusk approaches. Cautiously, warily, the interloper keeps eyes peeled skyward and tiptoes forward.

Stomach churning in anticipation, beads of newly created sweat stand out on the trekker's brow. He slowly advances, one cautious step at a time. Somewhere in the distance, vocal thrushes in residence chirp knowingly with one another. A stranger is in their midst. What are they saying to each other?

Is this woodlot a world unto itself? Perhaps it is a gift of the original creation? The light briefly reappears from the north. Not east or west? The north? Has the earth deviated from its axis? Thrushes swirl about

20

disoriented, confused, in a state of panic.
Their voices become shrill and panicky. Some
fly blindly into the trunks of trees, then drop
to the forest floor.

The traveler remains at peace. A
calmness mystically envelopes, then protects
his inner self. Beads of sweat on his brow dry
themselves. Worries quietly exit from this
psyche. What is this supernatural power which
claims ownership of his soul? What is this
mystical power that seems to impact birds
differently than humans? Are we indeed one
with nature? What if this relationship changes
and is no longer true? Mind boggling, this
questions a basic tenant of life on earth.

Scary!

A series of contemplative questions
rise to the surface. Could there have been
multiple creators? Is it possible that our
ecosystems are changing before our eyes?
Perhaps humankind is not the superior being?
Who else occupies this planet we call Earth?
The questions give him pause. It's not the first
time he has explored queries about the essence
of life. Evaluating his sanity while considering
the believability of the Creator is good for the
soul. Perhaps this is a test of survival.

The light in the paranormal forest
follows then suddenly leaps ahead in front of

the intrepid hiker. How is this possible? Where is this oracle of the planets taking him? An uneasy feeling tells him that there is another strange ecosystem residing in the marsh. Surrounded by water, marshy weeds and a fog-like mist, there is no escaping this strange place.

Desperately searching for a familiar frame of reference, he wonders if the multicolored skylights painted across the horizon are real. Perhaps this is a disillusionment in his harried and confused mind. A dream created just before he awoke? The desire to decipher the dream is fraught with fear, dread, suicidal temptations. The temptation to explain away the phenomena as imaginary, illusionary, or the product of derangement supersedes the determination to block our all analytical thought. Evaluating forces of creation which apparently exist outside our established knowledge, tradition, beliefs and cultures carries an equal amount of potential risk and reward. Is this heaven-sent light illusionary? Is God talking, or is there some otherworldly force?

Thoughts, ideas, concepts enter his psyche at unusual junctures. The forest lights cause him to pause, to evaluate who he is in relation to the quagmires on his journey. Are the lights real or imaginary? This deity-lead guidance carries him around the marsh. Is this an allegory for surviving the perils of life?

Sometimes a strange and unexplainable seer comes into our life and guides us to question the essence of what we truly believe. Can we be courageous? Can we take the risk and permit the docent in the forest to lead us to a heretofore unknown world of the third dimension?

Surprises await. God is the great I am. Be not afraid.

GOD'S COUNTRY

Snow covered, ice covered two lane macadam roads wind through the hillsides of Central Pennsylvania. A quartet of middle aged deer hunters are driving carefully due north to the long deserted Stoltzfus family farm in Perry County. An abandoned farm complete with a barn and corn crib, the rugged house with peeling paint has been used by these same men annually for nearly 25 years. Perhaps this is the year when a prized buck will be bagged.

A patch of black ice suddenly covers the pavement where long branched pine trees hide the sun's rays. Circling, higher and higher into the mountain range the Honda crawls at 25 mph. Knuckles turn white with anxiety as there are no guardrails, reflectors, or painted white stripes on the roadway's shoulders. An errant misjudgment and over the side tumbles the 2013 snow tire equipped Accord. The onboard navigation system grapples to keep up with the intersecting roads which suddenly appear from the hidden entrances to abandoned farms. The GPS' spoken directions are confusing and often useless. Not a comforting asset in this battle with winter's elements.

Narrow glimpses of mountain peaks sporadically emerge through open spaces in the fog covered windshield. The car's owner manual promised that fogging problems had been eliminated! Wrong again! So close, yet so far, we wishfully hope we are getting closer to the summit. Touchable? Not quite. Reachable with an hour or two of cautious driving? Perhaps. The V-8 engine groans after being restrained for hours. The car's engineers apparently hadn't taken formidable challenges like this into their design calculations.

Sam Stoltzfus, grandson of the farm's original owner, guesstimates the arrival time at Blain, PA. to be about 3 hours. Five hours later and the snowy peaks still beckon far in the distance. With the sun sliding behind the horizon, we can no longer clearly see the highway's shoulders. Loose gravel pings off the car doors telling us that the deep drops into the valley below are precariously close to the car's driving trajectory. This mountain road is not intended to be tourist country. Steep hillsides prevent the construction of rest stops. Legs crossed, we desperately need a toilet break plus a place to stretch and relieve increasing anxiety.

Reaching the summit to view God's grandeur on display wrongfully appears within reach. Appearances are deceiving. Another lesson in learning to be patient is delivered on a not-so-silver platter. Fervent prayer for a safe journey replaces macho conversation. Compatriot Mennonite and Reformed Christian travelers find common psalms to sing. The Honda Accord becomes a type of gospel chapel. The tension level among the hunters is rising and palpable. As darkness approaches, a sign in the shape of an arrow, nailed to a telephone pole, faintly points to" Stoltsfus." Weary riders take a deep breath as the reliable Accord navigates a left turn into the gravel covered farm lane.

A restful night of sleep on straw tick mattresses at the deer camp gives way to the welcoming rays of mid morning sunshine. Black coffee and greasy eggs are served for breakfast. YES! A man's cholesterol driven meal. Morning progresses and the lifting of the damp fog reveals the remnants of a washed out logging path winding its way through the farm yard clearing and into the base of the mountain. Bowed mulberry trees line the lower portion of the logging trail. Straining for many winters under the weight of wet snow and Pennsylvania's well known ice storms, the trees survive and provide food for the multiplying white tailed deer population. The logging trail leads to the eastern slopes of the Perry County Mountains. These slopes are almost impassable as a result of damages wrought by an infamous tornado striking the area in the spring of 1958. Fallen trees and gnarled bushes hide boulder-sized limestone rocks. Climbing is prohibitive. Are we seeing nature's revenge for man's incursion into this sanctuary? The locals believe this to be an obvious truth.

Alternatively, a secondary logging path leads to the more friendly western slope. Here is a bountiful home for wild turkey, white-tailed deer, black bear dens, and ever present beaver clans. The wonderment of the region's ever changing forest scape is evident to the infrequent, yet knowledgeable observer. Wildlife adapt, survive and prosper in ever changing circumstances. New sources of food and shelter were created after the tornado. Animals which once coexisted became cannibalistic food sources for each other in order to survive. White-tailed deer avoided their long used pathways down the mountainside. Harsher, colder winters thinned the herd. Only the strong survived.

His Nordic seafarer beard glistens in the sun. Shoulder length black and white salted hair blows this way and that. The aging patriarch of the mountain's residents extends a welcoming smile standing like a proud imperial landowner on the cutout margins of the power line trail. Hands outstretched, he warmly greets the yearly visitors to his homestead. Three generations on both sides of these families sustain an informal brotherhood. A cup of strong coffee with a touch of Jameson is passed around as the annual male bonding ritual begins. Humming "Born in America," Sam Stoltzfus faces southward and spies the outline of the beaver colony near where he long ago bagged his first antlered buck. Eyes watering, he recalls long forgotten youthful roots. Memories return of teenage hunters' frozen faces braving horizontally blowing snow. Cold hands and freezing feet in subzero temperatures made it difficult to release the 30-30 Winchester's safety and squeeze off a perfect shot? Will the buck bolt from the woods onto the grassy plateau? Watery, tear filled eyes and memory tapes recall the PLACE. It was a barren woodlot adjacent to the beaver dams.

A rustling sound in the bush broke the silence. One shot, then two reverberate off of the forest glen. Success! The wounded deer staggers and falls to its death on the grassy field. Sam, at age 14, became a man with this first deer kill. Then there was the gutting of the bleeding, downed deer. Remembered, at age 54, are the smells, sounds, and cheers of his fellow hunters as they stood and watched his hands probe for the liver and heart inside the carcass of the dead buck. Sam successfully

28

fought the urge to vomit. That would have been public, humiliating proof of his being a weakling.

Deer camp teaches the braggadocio arts of talking big, learning to drink beer and playing seven card stud poker. Following a long held custom, the tail of Sam's hunting shirt had been ceremoniously cut off with a hunting knife the previous season by the camp's elders. He had shot at and missed a deer. No matter that it was a difficult shot in dense brush. Sam humbly and with embarrassment nailed his shirt tail to the wall. How proudly the faded Woolrich shirt still hangs on the cabin's kitchen wall. Father and grandfather tell and retell legendary camp tales. Tradition is important.

Glints of the early morning sun on the second day reveal recent deer tracks in the snow. A doe and her fawns passed here during the long winter night. Additionally, sporadic yellow urine spots dot the winter snow near deer rubbed saplings. Evidence points to a healthy and well populated herd.

Preserving nature's gifts is a sacred trust. We are obligated to learn her language and the signs of where the wildlife live. Mid-afternoon quickly approaches and the winter sun begins to descend behind the mountain ridge as dusk approaches. Austrian wood knobbed walking stick in hand, the patriarch tracks the trail as it leads downwards to an ice covered brook. This familiar waterway has led more than one lost hunter out of the mountains on a dark, wintry afternoon. I was one of those disoriented hunters. Scared? Yes I was scared. Thanks to God for the mountain stream.

Ice is painfully coating the hiker's eyelids, but there is more to discover before we retreat to our cabin. Nighttime deer beds abound in the pine stand. Now cold from the previous night, a flattened matting bed beneath the trees reveals a favorite bedding site. Delightful memories of tracking deer in the snow to their nighttime beds return. However, today is a live and let live hike. We will not disturb the deer. Quietly and respectfully we exit by following the stream to a well traveled deer path near the cabin's rustic entrance. Let the deer and the animals of the mountain sleep peacefully tonight.

An inspiring hike into the past is too soon complete. Nature is patient. She knows our children. The next generation of caretakers will arrive next winter to again enjoy God's Country. Like us and our forefathers, they hopefully will leave the woodland unspoiled. We respectfully place a

30

stone marker on the hillside adjoining the beaver dam. Time has come to share our thanks for this beautiful countryside and pledge that the best of the past is again persevered. The next generation has been taught the love of this place. Yes, the locals are right. God has created and maintained this beautiful landscape. Let nature sleep and enjoy her beauty in revered silence.

INNER STRENGTH

It's a typical fall weekday afternoon in the frenetic, neighborhood Starbucks. Keyboards are gently tapped as sales types compose marketing letters. University students concentrate on writing theses about local hero Abraham Lincoln. Harried techno-geeks impatiently utter audible vulgar epithets while waiting in line for their daily latte. Business as usual: almost.

Clutching a high-end Coach computer case, she auspiciously enters via a side doorway, and glides across the sparkling clean tile floor. While displaying a purposeful demeanor, the stunning marketing executive checks her i-Phone for messages while stealthily gliding to the back of the take out line. Laptop users hesitate and awkwardly peer over their Apple screens. Students, gray haired guys, accountants pretend to be coy while furtively glancing in her direction. The glances soon change to all so obvious stares.

Wait staff take a deep breath, and smile at each other with the knowing look that communicates familiarity amongst their team. Each has seen this movie before as this singularly attractive femme fatale enters the cafe. A palpable atmospheric change occurs with patrons holding their collective breaths in fascination and awe of the newest arrival.

This elegant customer radiates the rare chemistry of charisma. Classy, perfectly attired like a model stepping out of Vogue, she wears Tiffany jewelry and shoes from Ferragamo. Not a common sight in dairy land USA. Time is suspended in this small town coffee shop. An unspoken question hangs in the air: "What mystical vapors cause everyone to be involuntarily drawn to this woman?" Unpretentious, confident, aware of her beauty, she shares platonic eye contact with customers including the local mayor. He meekly sips a plain coffee while seated at a strategically placed window table. Not so coyly, he observes the coming and goings of those in his sphere of political influence.

The female executive is in command, or is it control? What creates this singularly unique aura? Stunning beauty often merits a double take. But this is a vapor of a different magnitude. God-given gifts construct an indescribable personage. A lifelong reservoir of inner strength was developed within a family of defined, unchallengeable values. A portion of the generations long credo includes being thankful for one's special gifts while denying the temptation to take advantage of others who are weak and frail and susceptible to temptation. The strength to fend off those who would manipulate her beauty for their animalistic satisfaction or to resist using her gifts for unearned personal gain is deeply ingrained. Faith places integrity and humility above easily accessible monetary gain and physical pleasure. Temptation is present every day, around every corner, at each business meeting.

A glimpse into her personal history reveals that beauty, charisma, charm and superior emotional intelligence have been constant companions. They shadow her 24/7. Successfully avoiding the pitfalls of the modern world, she uses this strength to avoid the twin devils of condescension and effete snobbism.

Leading community activism to help those less fortunate is a priority. Arm candy for corporate leaders at national fundraisers for the disabled, her charisma and charm bring well-heeled donors to contribute substantial amounts. Saturday mornings finds her dressed in jeans and sweatshirt, schlepping cartons of canned fruit from delivery trucks to the shelves of the local food pantry. It's a serious obligation to keep poor families from starving. Without God's gifts of charm and beauty she realizes her advantageous position in society may not be possible. Rubbing elbows with the town's poorest citizens, she clearly understand that what is given can be instantly lost.

Faith, yes it is faith that separates the gifted who share their personal treasures as opposed to those who are avaricious and selfish. Inner belief in the Almighty reinforces the desire to willingly extend her helping hands to those with emotional and physical needs.

She exits the Starbucks with latte in hand. Her gait communicates a sense of determined purpose. Today her God given gifts will again be used to make the world a better place.

SEASON

THE SINGLE LEAF

The front and back yards of our Wisconsin home feature eye-catching fifteen foot tall mature, red   maple trees. They are positioned prominently in order that my wife Agnes, daughter Theresa, and I can hold closely the memories of now deceased grandmothers. Knowing Agnes and I are on the downside of our earthly lives, we hope that these trees will display the beauty of God for generations to come. Yes, it is our way of sharing family history. We see this as a simple and meaningful gesture. Plant the trees, nurture them in the early years, and nature takes over.

For any species to survive in the Great Plains is a near miracle. For two maple trees to battle and successfully endure the harsh climes is amazing. Twenty-four months ago we stared out the kitchen window admiring the latest six inches of overnight snowfall. As always, the sturdy backyard maple survived the snow, ice, and 40 mph winds blowing south from the Canadian provinces.

A furled, fatigued singular leaf catches our attention as it remains attached to a spindly limb on Grandma Gress' otherwise barren maple tree in the backyard. Since the day of planting, this maple has displayed the strength, determination, fierce independence so evident in Grandma Gress' personality. The leaf hangs on displaying a determination reminiscent of Grandma herself. We call the tree the "Last Survivor". What is the message? Each wintry morning, steaming Colombian coffee in hand, Agnes and I stand arm in arm at the window to see if our friend ,the Single Leaf remains. Yes, December, January, February the leaf is still attached. What is the message? Is there a message?

We struggle to interpret what it is that Grandma Gress is saying? Is she reminding us about the importance of strength, perseverance, and religious faith? On a gray March 2013 morning we notice that the leaf is gone. Our friend has slipped away silently into the darkness of a frigid winter night. We feel the pings of regret. The Colombian coffee has a sudden chill. Will a surrogate leaf grow in its place next spring 2013?

This subsequent winter has seen 19 days of unrelenting snow in the first 23 days of December 2013. Temperatures are ten or more degrees below normal. Continuous, almost daily snow storms become the normal weather event week after week. The debilitating impact of continuous Arctic cold temperatures take their toll. With the leaf gone, we now apprehensively part the lace curtains in the kitchen and check to see if the driveway and deck are hidden with more of the Arctic wind driven snow. The surrounding forests and fields are void of leaves and green color. God takes us by the hand and leads us to the kitchen window to enjoy the beauty of His snow covered landscape.

Spring arrives in late April 2014. There it is again. A singular leaf comes before the others. Small, fragile, light green in color, it appears to be clinging for life. A relative of the furled brown leaf which captivated us last year (2013) beckons for our attention.

Like its predecessor, this fragile gift of nature survives the forces of harsh springtime storms. The leaf stares at us each time we look out the window. Is the red maple's garment smiling at us? Are we dreaming or seeing a product of our imaginations? God blesses us again. Fervent prayers for healing and perseverance have been heard and answered by God again and again as we have endured medical and other challenges in the four months since being greeted by our first leafy visitor. This second generation leaf reaches out and encourages us to continue to pray, to have faith.

A freak of nature? Accidental Just a coincidence? We believe those with little faith may have a difficult time explaining away this remarkable happenstance. It is time for us to pray, listen, meditate. We have been blessed. May we welcome the spirit that brings the leaf back into our lives and tells us what is needed.

Perhaps the maple tree's leaf knew it was under observation. Undaunted by the tribulations of horrific winter storms, the leaf courageously clings to the tree. The leaf communicates that people need to watch what they do and hear and what is said every day. Our strength, tenacity, faith in the Almighty (or lack thereof)are on display as we observe our companion from behind hand sewn Belgian lace curtains. We are expected to provide examples for others in order that they too may have positive guideposts to follow.

THE SOUNDS OF RAIN

The tapping sound of tiny ballet slippers gleefully resonate as they parade against the kitchen window panes on a rainy spring morning. Listen! They are bringing messages. The gnomes of the storm speak to us. They whisper what we need to hear: in sync with our mood and temperament. Yes, each set of musical rain symphonies is designed to influence the internal stories of our personal history. We watch the drops dance down the panes and realize that rain talks to us in a language unique to us as individuals. We are consumed by the desire to understand who we are, why are we here? What does this moment mean?

Where were you when the life changing rains came and your values were questioned to the core? Perhaps you were reading a mind expanding book? Or interacting with a mentor who motivates you to become more than you ever imagined? Maybe the love of your life appeared out of nowhere? Was there a specific time when your faith life became a real, living part of who you are deep in your soul? Essential to the nurturing of the very plants that sustain each of us, rain, the carrier of nutrients for Mother

40

Earth is also a carrier of our moods, creativity, values and lifestyle choices.

When we choose to listen, we have an opportunity to hear life giving life. We can invite the rain which is pelting against the kitchen windows to come inside our mind and chat with the most private caverns of our soul. Yes, we must first grant the messenger permission. What we do with those messages are personal choices. Being open to the wisdom of the Creator of rain frees us to visit our garden of life. Cleansed, refreshed, we have an opportunity to root out the destructive weeds in our life. Hoeing and fertilizing our personal garden provides air and nutrients for future growth and our capability to serve others.

The cycle of personal rain followed by cleansing, productive action, and reexamination of the soul repeats itself forever. These are gifts from God to help us move forward. Likewise, we have an opportunity to help our brothers and sisters with the challenges of planting and sustaining their own personal gardens. Alternatively, we can choose to permit the rains to overwhelm us. To let the weeds of distraction and self destruction drown our souls in disgust. Yes, this is a conscious choice. A choice based on who we have decided to become.

We have a chance to be more, share more, love more. It's a decision we have the opportunity to make many times a day. Delight in the self sculpture of who you want to be.

THE GIFT OF A WINTER

STORM

Password needed? How secretive we have become, i Pad, i Phone, Blackberry, the list goes on. Skype, Messenger, videoconferencing, innumerable ways of communicating. Electronically guided drones are watching over us, around us, everywhere. Technology is amazing as was man's long ago discovery of how to make fire. How far humankind has progressed!

The Long Island Expressway is a morass of inactivity. Cars are strewn helplessly like so many erratic Lego blocks. Experts on the weather channel predict lots of snow. The forecasters postulate for days on end.

Four wheel drive turbocharged vans are designed to carry us over mountains and through rough terrain - isn't that what the ads say? So much for truth in advertising. Days later and county snow plows continue the struggle to reclaim highways from the clutches of Mother Nature.

Irony? Techno marvel drones can take detailed pictures of our continental storm fronts. However, we are powerless to slow down the impact of these oncoming blizzards. Helpless, we sit in front of the fireplace and wait and wait and wait while enduring the latest weather related challenge. Snow falling in horizontal waves blurs the vision as we peer out the bay windows. The TV is inoperative. Thank goodness a roaring fire keeps us warm and projects a warm fuzzy protective feeling.

Here's an opportunity to ignore cabin fever and contemplate without man-made interference. If we listen, really listen, the Spirit talks to us amongst the swirling sounds of wintertime gales while snow lashes against the thinly insulated walls of humble homes. Yes, He is in our midst listening to our prayers and thoughts while holding us safe during these scary times. Surprisingly, we are provided an opportunity to avoid spending our valuable hours watching mindless TV cooking shows, soap operas, and reality shows. Storms provide an alternative when the electricity is cut off. Power lines are strewn across the interstate highway as trees break like so many toddler toys. Instead of complaining about the inconveniences, we can take time to ponder the truth set forth by learned scholars and the Gospels. Prayer and meditation await our attention.

Let's put aside the Internet and engage the TVs off button and discontinue living at a

44

frenetic pace. Now is the time to enjoy the quiet which comes with the shrinking world outside. Snowdrifts surround our homes while wind driven snow piles up against the front door and barricades us inside. An overstuffed chair, roaring fire, scented candles, perhaps a cup of Irish Coffee all combine to create an inviting venue for us to reflect, seek insight, share with each other the wisdom of St. Francis of Assisi. These wintry interruptions are a blessing which can be used for our own higher purposes.

SNOWFLAKE FOR A

MOMENT

Fluttering, falling to the ground while riding the wind currents, the snowflake searches for a cold, isolated strand of brown grass. Alone, hidden and temporarily safe, she knows the length of her sojourn near Ephraim is brief. Transformed this January morning from solid ice to soft flaky snow, she is perfect in so many ways. Designed by the greatest artist of all times, there are many like her. Her friends gather around to assist in dazzling the countryside. Clones of each other, they coexist and then ultimately perish together.

Her brilliance flashes momentarily before the eyes of even the most casual tourist. No one knows her, yet everyone is dazzled. They want to cradle this frigid, diamond-like creation in the palm of their hand. Evidence of God's magic seems to rest in their midst. Snuggled alone near the base of a leafless cranberry bush, she knows the expedition is quickly ending. She has delivered her message of beauty and creation to all who would see. Hiding is not an option. The sun relentlessly searches for her. There is no way to disappear, no place to hide for protection. The end is inevitable. Melting begins to return her to the form she knew as cold water in a former life. Beautiful, frozen and alone, she lays unprotected.

Would her life giver return and perform magic again? Would she be recreated to beautify another Door County hillside? A beautiful snowflake, she was created to cover the barren and deserted woodlands and to be enjoyed by all of God's creatures. Can this magic act be repeated?

She gave everything to be a vital part of nature's artistry. Peace comes as the sun warms the grass. The ultimate gift is at an end.

TRADITIONS TO BE

CHERISHED

A not so typical craft room in a Virginia Veterans Administration hospital is alive with determination and dedication. The autumn fall has arrived with maple trees in their fall multicolored glory. Para professional staff flit about in starched white uniforms preparing coffee, hot chocolate along with half gallon containers of newly pressed apple cider. Tables of chocolate chip cookies, polish donuts, and cream puffs await the soon to arrive veterans. This is a special time of the year. Time when these vets prepare to once again give to others by creating cherished Christmas figurines.

Slim pipe cleaners, bottle cap tops, party glitter, odds and ends from craft kits are jumbled together in the bottom of a crumpled cardboard box. First created more than 50 years ago by WW II veterans, each completed figurine carries a story, a history. Their past is connected, as if by magical osmosis, through the artistic hands of aging, injured veterans, any of these heroic soldiers from the battles in Korea, Vietnam, Iraq and Afghanistan live with nightmares and memories of horrific events. Even while struggling with

48

amputations and Post Traumatic Stress Disorder these men and women are determined to once again give back to others.

Backs arched, shoulders bowed, they bend over tables lined with trays of craft supplies. Each man and woman proudly strives to create mystical Christmas decorations. Twitching fingers struggle to attach glue to paste stars and snow at exactly the desired spot. The desired facial expression is a necessity.

The craft room's air is filled with a cacophony of laughter as veterans loudly brag about their grandchildren who visit on weekends. How proudly they show off their lovingly created dancing figurines. Quieter chatter periodically engulfs the room as the battlefield deaths of buddies are recalled. A reverent atmosphere surrounds these artisans. Wonder what each vet is thinking?

Survivors of our nation's finest generation spend some of their final days in this hospital. A cadre of caring medical personnel unselfishly provides the care and love so rightly deserved. These heroes cherish their last days with brothers in arms. Who knows what the morning sunrise will bring? Who will pass away during the long winter night? Esprit de corps lives on.

Each Christmas season these handcrafted figurines find their reserved spot on the window sills of homes both modest and grand. A special place is reserved for these works of art. Decades pass and the citizenry continues to pay homage to those who sacrificed so very much.

Several figurines were carefully crafted by a vet who subsequently served as a chef at this Veterans Administration Hospital. Then an illness felled him and he transition from being an employee to that of a hospital resident. After a decade of proudly serving his country in the hospital's kitchens, he gave his life. The chemicals present in cleaning materials used to cleanse sinks, ovens, etc. are believed to have possibly destroyed his body in the form of leukemia. Another member of the greatest generation quietly, humbly succumbed. His grave at a quiet church cemetery is marked these four decades later by an American Flag and a stone memorial. The Veterans Hospital's entrance has a bronze plaque displaying the names of those who gave the ultimate sacrifice. My wife's father's name is proudly listed there and will remain forever.

The figurines were found discarded in a long forgotten cardboard box along with other mementos in his widow's attic. Strange how the Lord knows which mementoes tug at our heartstrings. His gift of the figurines provides us a lifeline to the past which will be passed along to the next generation.

This attic was a family museum that provided tangible means of retaining our country's traditions and history. Absent of blinking lights, gaudy jewels, these simplistic, crude figurines remind us of the sacrifices made for us. The figurines have now been passed to our generation. The annual unpacking of Christmas mementoes including the figurines is a moving, emotional, reflective time. It's a tradition which speaks louder and louder as we grow in years. A tradition of remembrance, of family loyalty which we pray will be continued by our children in years to come.

Much of Christmas season's celebrations revolve around tradition. Be it decorations, favorite foods, or attending church together, families repeat what has been cherished and passed on by each generation. Traditions have a way of keeping families close while remembering those who are deceased. Indeed, these special times are unique and sacred to each family.

SELF

EXPLORING OUR LIFE'S

PURPOSE

Consider this an invitation. A solicitation if you will. Today is a perfect time to think the extraordinary. A time to consider a question worthy of the practical minded and the ephemeral philosopher. While the query is timeless, responses are unique to your individual culture, values and current life circumstances.

Pause and in the privacy of your inner self, explore a concept which deserves undivided attention. The only provisions needed for this journey are time, patience and self -honesty.

*Time… to spend wisely and concentrate without regard for what comes next on your daily calendar.

*Patience… make the decision to temporarily halt the onrushing flood of decisions facing you. Pause, take a breath and believe in yourself.

*Honesty… enjoy the reflection of your face in the mirror. Listen to the sound of your breath. Consider whether or not these two elements combine to create the honest you.

The spelunking of the mind takes us into an inner sanctum filled with awe and wonder. A place infrequently visited. This is a mystical yet cherished venue open to the opportunity for exploration of our inner self. There is a sense of welcome from spiritual guides who gently beckon our movement beyond lifetime constructed walls of self-protection. These barriers keep us focused on down-to -earth day-to-day events while preventing us from considering what really makes us who we are. A flashing directional sign appears at an intersection as we enter our cavernous mind. The sign points to the seemingly safe path of our usual responses to life's challenges. Well worn, we have been here many times. We know the routes which keep us comforted and happy. The second sign is vague. A road which is less traveled. The small, faintly painted directional sign beckons us to take decision making risks. The future lies down this road. We are aware of an inner voice whispering the rhetorical question:

"WHAT DO I LIVE FOR?"

Let us not be tempted by the contemporary psychobabble terms "motivation", or "drive". Turn the exploration light brighter and more focused. Meditate in a comfortable manner while allowing yourself to follow the dimly lit highway which leads to the examination of factors which are highly personal.

"WHAT DO I LIVE FOR?"

The nagging question is repeated and repeated. Have a ready answer? Money, clothing, trips to the Bahamas? Really? Is personal pleasure the rationale of why God placed you here on earth? Are luxury, self-indulgence, ego-centered activities a central part of God's plan?

Look into a mirror for self-reflection. Take your time. There is no rush. Relax and concentrate on the visage before you. This is an opportune moment to take a second or third look. How can we silence the ever growing loud voice which praises our materialistic responses? What does God want from us? Pause, meditate. Yes, introspection can be a bit uncomfortable. We can't stop looking in the mirror. Deception is not possible. It is time for an extreme makeover.

The mirror asks: " What about your special talents"? Are you using them to cleanse your soul so that you can do good for others outside of your insular self? Relinquishing personal, ego driven, unnecessary trifles is

54

necessary to be able share our talents: to address the needs of our children, our parents, the poor, the disoriented, for the betterment of family and country. The mirror and prayer are our two foremost allies in this time of difficult self-examination. At times the mirror feels like an adversary pulling us down an unmarked road of decision making and commitment.

Whatever response you ultimately choose may evoke visceral feedback. Sweating hands, a nervous fluttering in the stomach, shaking from within, are caused by the uncertainty of exploring our inner self. The inner voice could be yelling: "YES! " This is why I am here. I am going to reshape my life to include a newfound purpose for myself and others be they loved ones or strangers.

Take a risk. Share this truth with someone who you discuss intimate secrets. They will see you in a different light." What has happened to you?" They may ask. A new sense of trust develops when we join with others to walk this heretofore undiscovered trail.

Trust yourself and others. God placed us here for a purpose. Remember the self-discovery of St. Francis of Assisi? He gave up his earthly riches to help others. Like St

Francis, enjoy the fascinating, fulfilling journey of exploring these most private of all inner caves which can make you a special person.

THE WONDERMENT OF SELF-

DISCOVERY

A muggy humid day at the Monet--like flower covered preserve near ancient lakes surrounded by soaring green hemlocks in the hills of Northern Wisconsin finds adults scrambling for shade, natural ice tea, or a Budweiser. A lone child dashes through the prairie grass. Her curiosity never stops to rest.

Flowers, bushes fallen red maple trunks present a new adventure park for this young nymph. Rising to her waist and beyond, long stems of yellow stalks greet her eye to eye. An ethereal hello, how are you? Curiosity welcomes golden wildflowers which are this girl's first encounter with Mother Nature in the wild. An audible sigh of delight flows out of the bed of wildflowers. Indeed, a shriek of glee and amazement reverberates down the river glen. She stretches her tiny fingers and gently caresses the waiting bouquet. Flower and child seem to carry on a conversation. Intense, passionate, innocent, playful, the beginning of a lifetime relationship with nature is consummated in a millisecond.

Elderly adults lovingly observe the newfound curiosity of their grandchild.

Watching with self-satisfaction their values are passed on to another generation. Wizened septuagenarians marvel at the pure, innocent joy being shown by their granddaughter along with her respect for Mother Earth.

Our memory tapes speed back through the decades attempting to recreate similar feelings we displayed at age 2 or 3. Each encounter recalls a long forgotten jewel placed on their dresser for admiration by grandparents past. The understood obligation in each scenario is to care about nature and one another. The little lady in the prairie grass is grasping these long held values.

While reclining on backyard decks, elders collectively solve the world's problems, tell tales of accomplishments and times past, as well as their love for the latest nature officiando in the family. A tradition continues.

Upon identifying solutions to any of life's problems, do we proclaim a youthful Ah-ha when there is a sense of discovery, and a return to innocence? Do we hear the internal songs of joy, and experience a heart pounding thrill like a 3 year old climbing over fallen tree limbs and running into waist high prairie grass?

Let us be free to listen to nature
and the joys of our inner child's
memory.

GIVING OF YOUR TIME

Horace Mann, in an 1859 commencement speech at Antioch College, exhorted the graduating seniors to "Be ashamed to die until you have won some victory for humanity." This is   a powerful challenge. Words similar to these have undoubtedly reverberated off the walls of many a liberal arts college auditorium on graduation day. We hear a challenge to do more than simply participate, more than to give of our largesse; more than being part of the cheering throngs on the streets demonstrating for this cause or that. Mann urges us to use our God-given talents to make a difference in the lives of others.

To win implies a sense of commitment on our part. The challenge is to advance an idea, policy, or cause that you believe will make a difference. Yes, we are called upon to be an agent of significant change in which we REALLY believe. Reflecting upon our core values and traditions, what is lacking or amiss in society that we want to modify? Meaningful, long lasting, impactful change involves taking risks. Change agents dismiss the axiom "To get along, go along." Inventors, doctors, philosophers, religious leaders who make a difference find that being

on the cutting edge can be quite lonely.
Maintaining the status quo is comfortable.
Like-minded thinkers support us. Focus
groups applaud our efforts. Do we really want
to climb out on a fragile limb and be all alone?
This can be an uncomfortable existence.

Consider the sacrifices of Abraham
Lincoln, Nelson Mandela, Mother Theresa,
Martin Luther King Jr., Jesus Christ, Mahatma
Gandhi. Each had a profound impact on
humanity. Some paid the ultimate price. They
died for their beliefs, taking risks while acting
upon the precepts that stoked the fire in their
belly to make a difference in the human
condition. While we do not need to sacrifice
our lives to be a change agent, there is a
necessity to be different, to swim against the
current. Change implies new ways of thinking,
developing new technology, looking askance
at how the world currently exists. Remember
the "different" kids who stood apart from the
rest during our school days? He or she may
have been a genius, a radical thinker, someone
who dressed differently. They stood out. Do
we want to mirror their social standing? Have
a desire to be the first in your social group to
defy the norm? Or is your legacy to be
someone who used their gifts and talents to fit
in, to be one of the crowd, to succeed without
making a difference? These are not easy
decisions.

Certainly, those with superior intellect such as Jonas Salk, Madam Curie, Pasteur, Dr. Yanish Pannu, and others have made this a better, safer, healthier planet. The common thread in this group is they all sacrificed time, effort, and many of the comforts in life to invest their time in medical advances. The axiom, "nothing in life is free" applies. Are we willing to sacrifice time with our families, perhaps moving to another country, setting aside the time we want and need to spend with our families? What matters to you that you will leave this world without taking a risk to stir the pot: to put your reputation on the line? Are you willing to give of your time, knowledge, and skills to help make this a better place?

This in no way is intended to minimize the gifts that those like the Pettit's have bestowed in Milwaukee, or Bill and Linda Gates, or the Annenberg Foundation. For most of us it is not possible to parallel the giving power of these generous philanthropists. However, as Fr. Dan Sanders says, give of our substance, not our excess. This applies to talent, courage, ideas as well as monetary gifts. Mother Theresa was a fitting modern day role model who leveraged courage, strength, and political skill for the greater good.

Each of us has the opportunity and obligation to share our talents in ways which can benefit others. Take a moment and consider what others admire about you. Is it your ability to listen to others? How about the capacity to teach by being a mentor, guide, role model for young or old? The gifts given to us by our Lord to share with others are endless.

To use our time exclusively for our own benefit is a selfish tragedy. We all have a chance to help others have a better life by selflessly sharing our gifts and talents. Sitting and sharing of your time with an elderly person may seem like a minor gesture of kindness. Yet, to a lonely person who lives alone or in an assisted living community, you are giving them the priceless gift of companionship. The sharing of your time may be the singular most impactful gift you can give.

Won't you share your time and talents?

THE PRIDEFUL DAYS OF

RETIREMENT

When one reaches the final entries on the insurance company's life expectancy table, it can be a time for serious reflection. Statistically, we see the approaching darkness as signaling the inevitable end of life on earth. We ponder decades of what was, what could have been, and reminisce about acquaintances, loves and past adventures. We stifle tear-jerking emotions while reviewing Christmas card lists containing increasing red line cross outs as friends and relatives pass on. Lists of the living become shorter with each successive advent season. We consider ourselves fortunate when cards continue to arrive from lifelong friends. Handwritten notes tell prideful stories of successful grown children, grandkids, and retirement villages. Absent is the palpable excitement associated with ski trips, career success, vacations to Europe and Asia. Life stories now recount recollections rather than future aspirations.

Cocktail parties and church social gatherings now often begin with the predictable query, "How is retirement?" Friends inquire with empathetic, sometimes pain laced tones conveying a not- so- subtle message: Sorry you are getting older. "I hope it has been a good life and you are feeling well." The explicit inference is they are sorry the end is near as we all approach the Pearly Gates. A reflective question for consideration:" Do we take time to look into life's mirror and enjoy the good times by reflecting on the many blessings we have enjoyed, the people we have known, and the insights we have been fortunate to share with others?"

Alternatively, have we made a conscious choice to exist on the darker side of the river Styx? Are we a living example of "dead man walking" wherein we have grown old physically and mentally? Our eyes have that distant lost look. The ravages of time have beaten us into submission and we have become iconic examples of grumpy old men and women. The choice to remain vibrant can be difficult. Are we to be old physically and mentally, or "spirited"? It's a choice which separates the grouchy from the senatorial. To give in is to give up.

Retirement is an opportunity to recognize an accumulation of knowledge and experiences and use them as a basis for reveling in the memories of the past while creating new adventures to which we have previously aspired. Our bucket list is always revisable. Now is the opportunity to fill up the bucket with new ideas. By the way, what life picture do you see others painting of you? Does it matter what others think? Only we know the recipe for our happiness. Why not feel free to dismiss other's evaluations and enjoy ourselves? Life's journey is unique for each of us. Perhaps we can pound our chest and let out a Tarzan yell with pride and joy. Retirement can be a celebration of victories large and small.

Let us proudly wear the mantle of grace and pride, for we have accomplished and contributed much to the greater good by using the Lord's gifts.

AMNESIA'S DARKNESS

An earthy handshake is the public signature of this confident giant of a man who has proven that perseverance and faith lead the passage from the fragile existence of a poor, humble farmer to becoming the president of a very successful international manufacturing company. The strength of his vice-like grip handshake communicates friendship, loyalty, a recognition of lives shared together. Man to man love in its purest form. Oftentimes it's a two handed shake, a pat on the back, a jocular "How are you doing?"

Social gatherings with our friend have transitioned to a quiet event where we now patiently listen to his repeated reminiscences of years past. He recalls stories about the gallantry of his widowed mother, the challenges of building a business, dangers faced fighting in the Korean War. Friends of many decades pause at our Formica covered table at the small town diner during Sunday breakfast. They smile and offer an obligatory hello. Upon departure, a blank stare with expressionless silence crosses the puzzled face of our gentle friend. He poses a sad question which arises from the darkness of his soul: "What is their name?"

So it goes. This community leader and r friend struggles to hold on to reality while ing into the darkness of Alzheimer's e. Sometimes aware that his memory is disappearing, other times not. How does he cope?

Family and friends strive to maintain a positive, upbeat mood to hide their sadness. A family secret is created, to protect the community icon from the outside world. Each relative protects this saint of a man from the whispers of those who may suspect a personality change. Time passes and the enveloping darkness becomes more pronounced. The once glistening eyes now have the distant, vacant look of an explorer desperately searching for a familiar path down the mountainside.

What is our obligation to friends and family who are slipping away? Each day it becomes more difficult to identify a clear picture of who our friend is and what he is becoming. We desperately want to protect him from self injury, from the pain that comes with loneliness. Yes, we feel hopeless at being unable to stem the tide of increasing darkness and disorientation. Prayer appears to be our last refuge as we too retreat into sympathetic aloneness.

Every culture caresses, cuddles and protects the infants in their society. It is natural to embrace a newborn, no questions asked. Can we do any less for our aging, infirm brothers and sisters? Let us protect them despite our self-centered feelings of desperation and helplessness. Strongly supporting a friend in need of a caring hug, even when they don't know they are being helped is a moral obligation. The final clasping of a dying person's hand is a handoff to God that we all remember.

Christ said, "Bring the little children unto me." Age is not a factor. Fragility and dependence on friends and family may occur at any stage in life. Let us wrap our loving arms around those who need us as they find themselves helpless and descending into darkness.

RETIREMENT QUESTION–

WHO AM I?

After years of being employed, some retirees find themselves a bit disoriented, even lost. Some conclude that they are emotionally sapped of energy. Additionally, there has been the continuing challenge of complying with society's expectations. Comporting with these strictures imposed by others is sometimes an energy draining chore. Successful in many aspects of life such as accruing financial wealth, being a recognized leader, respected family man, our friend nevertheless feels an emptiness in that life is dictated by a reaction to circumstances beyond his control. Other people seem to control his destiny.

He has successfully navigated the turbulent waves of seizing business opportunities. The ability to comprehend the complexities of marketing new products and negotiating contracts sets him apart from competitors in the business community. A well respected proponent of servant leadership, employees respect and applaud his character. Employees describe him as honest, trustworthy, fair, a motivator, and an owner who strives to ensure security for everyone.

With a retirement account valued well into seven figures along with multiple homes, yachts, and complete financial freedom, there is no worry of going broke when the mind and body weaken. Religion? Yes, he admits to passively attending church once a month. It's a business networking opportunity. Church is a place to make and maintain contacts while keeping up appearances in the community. Plus it keeps his wife happy. But deep in his soul he knows his church affiliation is a blatant deception.

Accumulating material wealth has been his lifelong quest. All other objectives rank a distant second. Relationships with his family and his God are at the bottom of the list of what is deemed important. Traveling North America in search of customers, life sped by at a hectic, mind numbing pace. Hotels, restaurants, conference rooms began to merge and look alike. Pages on the calendar turned from month to month with increasing rapidity as the decades passed. There has not been time to pause, reflect, to meditate as to what else besides money might be important.

The time remaining before considering retirement is quickly diminishing. The clock of life ticks ever faster. He surveys the frost covered acreage of the multi acre estate from the steps of the mansion's grandiose front porch. The beauty of the snow covered Great Plains is awe inspiring. Nature has painted a breathtaking morning sunrise landscape. A mug of java in hand, he fleetingly entertains the thought that this would be a terrific place to rest, pause and meditate. Yes, if there was time. A question imploring him for a response "WHO AM I?" rolls across the pastureland. Defensively he shouts, "Go away! I don't have an answer. I don't want an answer."

Six decades have passed since leaving the successful life as a commodities trader in Lower Manhattan. Inventing an electronic scanner which attracted angel investors, freedom from the Big Apple beckoned. The low cost of labor and ideal transportation systems of Canada made moving to this quiet small town at the base of the Rocky Mountains a wise choice. Over the years, town officials and neighbors have grown to respect the Yankee adventurer. He is blessed with the unique capacity to be a "listener", to provide an empathetic ear, to understand what people are really saying, and to intuitively sense the needs of others. Town officials and employees see him as a leader who knows who he is and where he is headed. The general consensus: he's a perfect person who has the perfect life. An image of perfection cultivated carefully. Now a nagging question comes out of nowhere "WHO AM I?"

Accruing more "stuff", owning a McMansion, gaining political power, constant community visibility are recurring themes for success. Suddenly and astonishingly these things no longer seem important. For the first time since immigrating to Canada an emptiness in his inner soul asserts itself. Concurrently, migraines like thunderbolts resoundingly clap behind his eyes. Beads of nervous sweat dance on a freckled forehead while hands perspire, shake, tremble. For self protection, a walled -in world without confidants and loved ones shielded the entrepreneur from inquiring eyes. Alarmingly, there is now no one to confide in and share secrets, dreams, desires. No one to help answer the question "WHO AM I?"

The acres of pastureland and soybean fields spread out before him are a metaphor for vast nothingness. Quiet, alone, there is an absence of people, direction, anyone with whom he can confide. How about sharing with wife and children? No, they are strangers. Business partners? No, they are strangers. God? He has never needed God or spoken with Him. No, He is a stranger too. The end of life is approaching and loneliness darkens the horizon.

So smart, so successful, yet so alone. Sound familiar? A question hanging in the air

is do we have the courage and strength to seek
out the counsel of our Lord and those who
love us? The consequences of disappearing
alone onto a seemingly endless prairie without
seeking the truth to "WHO AM I?" engenders
fears of isolation and desolation. Conversely,
we have heard relatives and friends say before
they die "I am at peace, I am ready." These
calm souls sought and found the answer to
their question "WHO AM I?"

36990468R00046

Made in the USA
Lexington, KY
12 November 2014